WORLD IN VIEW
SOUTHEAST ASIA
Antony Mason

STECK-VAUGHN
L I B R A R Y
A Division of Steck-Vaughn Company
Austin, Texas

Library of Congress Cataloging-in-Publication Data

Mason, Antony
  Southeast Asia / Antony Mason.
    p.   cm.—(World in view)
  Includes index.
  Summary: Discusses the geography, climate, natural resources, religions, history, agriculture, tourism, traditions, politics, and environment of Southeast Asia.
  ISBN 0-8114-2447-2
  1. Asia, Southeastern—Juvenile literature. [1. Asia, Southeastern.] I. Title. II. Series.
  DS521.M36   1992
  959—dc20   91-24807
                                                    CIP AC

Cover: *The main temple at Angkor Wat, Cambodia*
Title page: *Shwe Dagon temple complex, Rangoon, Burma.*

Designed by Julian Holland Publishing Ltd

Typeset by Multifacit Graphics, Keyport, NJ
Printed and bound in the United States by Lake Book, Melrose Park, IL
1 2 3 4 5 6 7 8 9 0 LB 96 95 94 93 92

Photographic credits
Cover: Douglas Dickins, title page: John Renner, 7, 9, 11 Antony Mason, 13 Robert Harding, 14, 16, 19, 21 Antony Mason, 22, 24 John Renner, 28 Mary Evans Picture Library, 29 J. Allan Cash, 31 Mary Evans Picture Library, 33 Antony Mason, 39, 43 Popperfoto, 44 Robert Harding Picture Library, 48 J. Allan Cash, 50, 52 Robert Harding Picture Library, 53 Douglas Dickins, 54 Antony Mason, 56 J. Allan Cash, 58 John Renner, 59 Jennifer Johnson, 61 Antony Mason, 63 Douglas Dickins, 65 J Allan Cash, 67 Antony Mason, 69 Douglas Dickins, 72 J. Allan Cash, 73 Douglas Dickins, 76 J. Allan Cash, 78 Robert Harding Picture Library, 80 John Stathos/Robert Harding Picture Library, 81 Douglas Dickins, 82 Antony Mason, 84 JHC Wilson/Robert Harding Picture Library, 85 Robert Harding Picture Library, 88 Luca Invernizzi Tettoni Photobank/BKK/Robert Harding Picture Library, 91 Douglas Dickins, 92 J. Allan Cash, 93 Luca Invernizzi Tettoni Photobank/BKK/Robert Harding Picture Library.

Contents

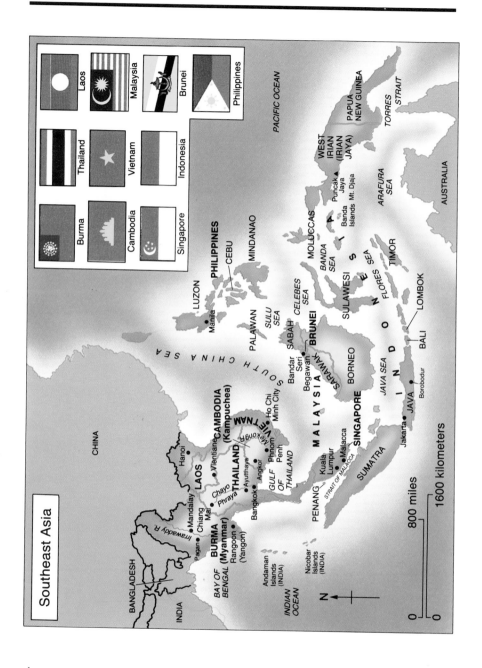

Southeast Asia

1   Land and Sea

Straddling the equator, in the tropical warmth of the South China Sea, lie a chunk of mainland Asia and a spattering of islands that have become known as Southeast Asia. Each of the ten independent countries of the region has its own history and traditions.

Across the region there is huge variety in landscape and in the people and their ways of life, from the forest peoples who live by hunting in remote mountains to the factory workers turning out computer microchips in the region's ultramodern business parks. Yet there are also many things that these countries have in common and that set Southeast Asia apart from other regions of the world and give it its own unique flavor.

This corner of Asia
The countries of Southeast Asia can be divided into two main groups. One is the mainland group, situated on the large piece of land attached to the rest of Asia and bordering India and China. The shape of this is sometimes compared to an elephant's head with its trunk hanging down. Burma (now officially called Myanmar), Thailand, Laos, Cambodia (also called Kampuchea), and Vietnam lie side by side in the north of this region, forming the head and ears of the elephant. These countries are sometimes referred to as Indochina. The Malay Peninsula forms the elephant's trunk, at the end of which lies the western part of Malaysia. At the very tip of

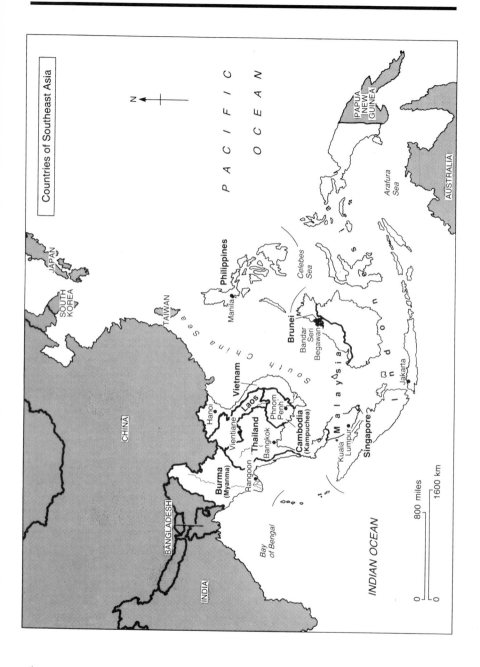

Countries of Southeast Asia

The exquisite landscape of Phang Nga in Thailand, on the west coast of the Malay Peninsula, is formed by massive weather-beaten limestone rocks rising straight out of the sea. The region is inhabited by ''sea-gypsies'' who build their villages on stilts over the sea, in the shelter of the rocks.

the trunk, crammed mainly onto one small island, is the independent state of Singapore.

Indonesia, a nation of 13,677 islands, forms the southernmost part of the region. The main islands are Sumatra, Java, and Sulawesi. Indonesia also shares the island of Borneo with the eastern part of Malaysia and the small independent state of Brunei. Half of the island of New Guinea also belongs to Indonesia and is called West Irian (Irian Jaya).

To the northeast of Borneo are the Philippines, a group of 7,100 islands, of which Luzon in the north and Mindanao in the south are the largest.

The total area of Southeast Asia, including the sea, is about twice that of the U.S. If you squeezed out all the water, however, you would have a landmass no greater than a third of the U.S.

The Countries of Southeast Asia

Country	Area	Population (million)	Capital	Main languages	Currency
Indonesia	782,660 sq m (2,027,087 sq km)	180	Jakarta	Bahasa Indonesia (a Malay-based language) and numerous local languages	rupiah
Burma (Myanma)	261,217 sq m (676,552 sq km)	38	Rangoon (Yangon)	Burmese and other local languages	kyat
Thailand	198,720 sq m (514, 820 sq km)	54	Bangkok	Thai	baht
Malaysia	127,581 sq m (330,434 sq km)	17	Kuala Lumpur	Malay, Chinese, English, Tamil	Malaysian dollar or ringgit
Vietnam	127,245 sq m (329,565 sq km)	62	Hanoi	Vietnamese, Chinese, French, English	dong
Philippines	115,830 sq m (300,000 sq km)	59	Manila	Pilipino, English, Spanish, and numerous local languages	peso
Laos	91,400 sq m (236,800 sq km)	4	Vientiane	Lao and local languages	kip
Cambodia	69,898 sq m (181,035 sq km)	6	Phnom Penh	Khmer, French	riel
Brunei	2,226 sq m (5,765 sq km)	0.25	Bandar Seri Begawan	Malay, Chinese, English	Brunei dollar
Singapore	239 sq m (620 sq km)	2.5	Singapore	Malay, Chinese, Tamil, English	Singapore dollar

A tropical climate

All of Southeast Asia except the very north of Burma lies in the tropics, that is to say, between the Tropic of Cancer and the Tropic of Capricorn.

These are two imaginary lines that lie 23.5 degrees to the north and south of the equator.

The tropics mark the farthest points north and south where the sun, at some point in the year, shines down from directly overhead. These are some of the warmest parts of the world. Southeast Asia has an average temperature of 82°F (28°C) throughout the year. It can be stiflingly hot, especially in the cities.

The coasts tend to be cooled by ocean breezes, making the climate there generally more comfortable. As the land rises up from sea level, average temperatures become more moderate. The hills and mountains are often used by wealthy people to provide a retreat from the heat of the lowlands; even at 4,920 feet (1,500 meters) you might need a sweater at night.

The people of Southeast Asia are quite used to the downpours that occur frequently during the wet monsoon. Rainstorms are usually short and sharp, so it is enough to find shelter until the clouds pass. For these vendors with their snack carts, a cloudburst brings a lull in their busy trade.

9

Monsoons and typhoons

Southeast Asia does not have spring, summer, autumn, and winter in the same way as the cooler regions of the world. Instead it has a wet season and a dry season. North of the equator the wet season lasts from about May to October; south of the equator the wet season lasts from about November to April. At the equator, the weather tends to be rainy most of the year.

We call the seasons of this region "monsoons," an old Arabic word meaning simply, "season." Although people often use the term to mean just the wet season, there is a dry monsoon and a wet monsoon.

During the wet monsoon it rains regularly, often in heavy downpours that turn country roads into mud. The air becomes very humid and sticky. This can be an uncomfortable time of year.

The wet monsoon is also the time of typhoons, vicious winds that build up over the sea, like the hurricanes of the Caribbean region. The Philippines are most affected by typhoons, suffering as many as 200 in a season. In October 1989, Typhoon Angela killed over 50 people and wrecked some 5,000 homes in the northern Philippines.

Beaches and tropical forests

There are all kinds of landscapes in Southeast Asia. There are the perfect little islands, with white sand beaches fringed with coconut palms, washed by a dazzling blue sea. There are the inland hills, coated with the deep green vegetation of tropical forest, or sculpted into hundreds of stepped terraces where the rice is

The stepped terraces of these flooded rice fields hug the contours of a steep hill. Such terraces represent a great feat of irrigation: each of the little fields has to be carefully connected to the supply of water. On each side of the neat terraces bamboo, coconut palms, and various other trees grow unchecked.

grown in flooded paddy fields. In the more remote regions there are coasts and inlets choked by the roots of millions of mangrove trees.

In the heat of this tropical landscape, the key to life is water. Where there are rivers or copious rain, the landscape will be richly green. This is not the case throughout the region. Many of the islands, such as Lombok and Timor in Indonesia, and some of the mountain plateaus suffer from the drought in the dry season, which leaves the landscape looking brown and rocky.

The great rivers

Rivers play a very important role in Southeast Asia, both as a source of water and as a means of communication. Where there are few roads, as in

11

northern Borneo, traveling by riverboat is the only means of reaching inland villages.

Southeast Asia's great rivers are all on the mainland part of the region. The Irrawaddy River flows the length of Burma, connecting the major cities of Mandalay and Rangoon, the capital (now officially called Yangon). In Thailand, the Chao Phraya flows from the northern hills through the city of Chiang Mai to the capital, Bangkok, in the south. Both of these rivers feed water to the rich rice-growing areas of the southern plains.

The greatest river of the region, however, is the Mekong, 2,598 miles (4,184 kilometers) long, the tenth longest river in the world. Rising in the mountains of Tibet, it flows through southern China, Burma, Laos, Thailand, and Cambodia before forming a great rice-growing delta as it flows into the sea in southern Vietnam. The river is of particular significance to Laos, a mountainous country, and the only one in the region without a coast of its own. The Mekong provides its main means of transportation.

However important they may be, these rivers are of questionable benefit in the wet season. They frequently spill over their banks and flood neighboring towns and farmland, causing widespread destruction.

A ring of volcanoes

Away from the coasts, the landscape of most of Southeast Asia rises quickly to rolling hills, and in some places quite high mountains. Mt. Djaja in West Irian is the tallest mountain in the region, at 16,500 feet (5,030 meters).

Southeast Asia also has numerous volcanoes.

The volcano Anak Krakatau, "son of Krakatau," is on an island between Java and Sumatra in the Sunda Strait. In 1883 Krakatau exploded in one of the most forceful eruptions ever recorded. Rocks and debris were hurled up to 34 miles (55 kilometers) away and the explosion caused a massive tidal wave which killed some 36,000 people.

They form a ring around the South China Sea. The Philippines has 30 active volcanoes, and Indonesia, with the most volcanoes in the world, has 70. The most famous of these is Krakatau, which lies between Java and Sumatra. Indonesia and the Philippines have so many volcanoes because they both lie along fault lines in the Earth's crust. The Earth's crust is made up of a series of plates that fit together like a jigsaw, holding in the molten center of the Earth. Whenever there is uneven pressure in the center of the Earth, its crust has to move or erupt to release the pressure. Indonesia and the Philippines lie along the line where the Pacific plate and the Indo-Australian plate meet, and so suffer from frequent tremors and eruptions.

The richness of the land

Southeast Asia is one of the most fertile regions of the world. With plenty of rain and rivers and a constantly warm climate, plants can thrive. Indonesia and the Philippines both have rich volcanic soil, while the great plains of mainland Southeast Asia are made extremely fertile by the mud swept down by the rivers. Farming is by far the most important occupation in the region. Rice, tropical fruits, coconuts, coffee and tea, sugarcane, corn, rubber trees, and oil palms are all grown on a large scale.

Gardens are filled with brightly colored flowers, such as hibiscus, bougainvillaea, orchids, and cannas. Many of the plants we grow as houseplants in colder climates, such as

The frangipani tree grows throughout the region and is famous for its beautiful blossom. Frangipani flowers have a scent that could justifiably be described as heavenly, and they are frequently used to decorate offerings and garlands in religious ceremonies.

poinsettias, and leopard lilies, grow wild, and often to a great size. The tropical forests contain teak, mahogany, ebony, and other valuable hardwoods. Logging is a major industry.

There are other riches beneath the soil. Tin, bauxite (used to make aluminum), copper, gold, coal, oil, and natural gas are all found in considerable quantities. The region is also one of the major producers of precious stones, particularly rubies, sapphires, and emeralds.

Natural variety
To match its variety of landscapes, Southeast Asia has a vast range of wildlife. Many of the species are what you might expect of tropical lands: butterflies and mosquitoes, lizards and snakes, birds of all colors and sizes, bats, deer, and monkeys. There are also honey bears, wild pigs, leopards, rhinoceroses, and crocodiles.

Southeast Asia also has many species of animals that are peculiar to it. The most famous is probably the orangutan, the large ginger-haired ape that lives in the forests of Borneo and Sumatra. Orangutans may look fierce, but they are actually quite gentle, living in small family groups and eating fruit, leaves, and honey. The name orangutan means "man of the woods" in the Malay language.

There are a number of interesting monkeys, including the crab-eating macaque, which inhabits the mangrove swamps; gibbons; and the extraordinary looking proboscis monkey of Borneo. The adult male has a long, fleshy nose, or proboscis, through which it produces a strange honking call.

15

Another famous animal is the huge monitor lizard called the Komodo dragon. It is only found on the small Indonesian island of Komodo and on a couple of neighboring islands. It is the world's largest lizard, growing up to 13 feet (4 meters) long. It eats wild pigs, deer, and goats, and has been known to attack and kill human beings.

There are many kinds of birds, from finches and parrots to eagles. The hornbill is a large black-and-white bird with a long curving beak, on top of which is a long hard "horn." When the female has laid her eggs, the male seals her into her nest by building walls of chewed mud around her, leaving just a slit through which he can pass food. Protected from tree snakes and monkeys, the female rears her young until they are old enough to fend for themselves.

Warm, shallow seas
Much of the sea in this area is comparatively shallow. The Sunda shelf, which occupies the

Fishing is one of the major occupations of the people of Southeast Asia. Simple fishing boats called outriggers are often made of just a hollowed-out tree trunk and floats consisting of long pieces of thick bamboo. These outriggers in Bali have been drawn up on a beach of black sand formed of fine grains of volcanic lava.

area bounded by Sumatra, Java, Borneo, and mainland Southeast Asia, averages only 120–180 feet (35–55 meters) deep. These warm, shallow seas provide an ideal setting for coral built by millions of tiny polyps. Living in and around the coral reefs are numerous varieties of fish. Many of these are beautifully colored and have equally colorful names, such as parrotfish, damselfish, angelfish, pufferfish. There are lobsters, crabs, jellyfish, and shellfish of all kinds, including the large, spiral-shaped chambered nautilus. In deeper waters there are tuna and sharks, and giant leatherback turtles.

2

Dynasties and Religions

Southeast Asia is often said to be at the crossroads of the world. In the early part of its history it formed the crossroads between the two great trading nations, India and China. Later it became the meeting point on trading routes to and from Europe, the U.S., South America, and Australia. Each of these routes brought with it new sets of people with new ideas, religions, and ways of life, all of whom have left their mark on the region.

Over the centuries, Southeast Asia has been carved up in different ways, as various kingdoms and empires grew and declined. The greatest empires built magnificent cities and temples. Parts of these have survived and rank among the world's finest historical monuments.

Java man

Around 500,000 years ago most of the islands of Southeast Asia looked very different. They were joined together by land, so it would have been possible to walk from Burma to the Philippines.

About this time an early form of human being, *Homo erectus*, lived in the region. We know this because remains of one of them was found in 1890 near the village of Trinil in Java. The discovery of "Java man" as he was called, showed that earlier forms of human life had existed before modern man, *Homo Sapiens*, emerged about 300,000 years ago.

Traders have been traveling across the South China Sea for thousands of years. The Bugis of southern Sulawesi operate the biggest working sailing fleet in the world, some 10,000 vessels. These Bugis schooners in the port of Jakarta are made in the traditional fashion, entirely of teak and without any metal nails.

About 5,000 years ago the first wave of people moved from southern China into the Malay Peninsula and throughout the Southeast Asian islands. These were the Malay peoples, who form the principal race in these regions today. Meanwhile other peoples of Chinese origin, notably the Thais, were beginning to settle in mainland Southeast Asia.

Trading nations

Mainland Southeast Asia was the site of some of the earliest metalworking cultures in the world, dating back to 3000 or 4000 B.C. A famous Bronze Age culture called Dong Son developed in northern Vietnam beginning about 1000 B.C. This culture spread from its base by conducting trade across the region and all the way down the Malay Peninsula as far as the island of Java.

By about A.D. 100 traders from two main neighboring nations, China and India, began to have a major influence on Southeast Asia. They would come to buy and sell spices, wood, minerals, precious stones, metalwork, pottery, and silk.

It would be another 1,200 years or more before the first Europeans set foot in this region, but trade links had already begun to connect East and West. Spices and silk reached the Roman Empire, either overland from China to the Mediterranean on the route known as the Silk Road, or across the sea to India and the Middle East, and then overland.

Hinduism

The Indian traders brought with them their ancient religion of Hinduism. Previously the people of Southeast Asia had been primarily animists, that is to say, they had local religions that worshiped nature and the gods and spirits that were believed to live all around them in trees, mountains, or water. The spirits of their ancestors were also often worshiped as gods.

India at this time had a wealthy, educated, well-ordered society in which Hinduism played a central part. The royal courts of Southeast Asia, therefore, were easily persuaded that Hinduism was a better, more sophisticated path. The central belief of Hinduism is that the world was created and is controlled by the gods, the best-known of whom are Brahma, Shiva, and Vishnu. The duty of all Hindus is to help maintain the order of

The elaborately decorated Buddhist temple of Wat Phrahat, near Chiang Mai, Thailand.

things, or *dharma*, by behaving correctly toward fellow human beings and toward the gods. After death they will be reborn, or reincarnated, as another being. If they behave well in one life they will be reborn as a better being in the next. After a series of good lives, the spirit or soul will be reunited with the Universal Spirit and achieve *nirvana*, or everlasting peace.

Hindu society is divided into four social classes, or castes, that are supposedly ordained by the gods. Strictly speaking, people have the caste of the family they are born into, and they cannot change it.

Buddhism
Trade with India later brought contact with another of India's great religions, Buddhism, which was spread by Buddhist missionaries

21

Statues of the Buddha are found in all the temples in Thailand. The Buddhas may be of solid gold or, more usually, of another material covered in layers of gold leaf. These are not gods to be worshiped so much as images of the perfect being, who has achieved nirvana *through meditation.*

throughout the Far East beginning in the second and third centuries A.D.

Buddhism was founded by an Indian prince named Siddharta Gautama who lived from about 563 to 483 B.C. He is known as Buddha, the enlightened one. His aim was to discover a way in which an individual could work to achieve *nirvana.* Buddha believed that human desire causes suffering and prevents us from finding nirvana. He taught that a life of quiet thought, meditation, and correct behavior can remove desire.

Buddhism shares much with Hinduism, including a belief in reincarnation, but it has no caste system. One form of Buddhism, called Theravada Buddhism, which has no god, was taken to Burma, Thailand, Cambodia, and Laos. Mahayana Buddhism, which includes a range of saints and Hindu-like gods, was taken to Vietnam by way of China. Elsewhere, as in Java, people followed what we now call Hindu-Buddhism.

Srivijaya and Sailendra

By the eighth century the first great empires of Southeast Asia were beginning to emerge. One series of empires developed on the mainland, while another developed in the islands and around the tip of the Malay Peninsula.

The Malay Peninsula and Sumatra are separated by a narrow channel called the Strait of Malacca. All the trading ships from India passed through this channel and met traders from China. Towns around the Strait developed into the great trading empire called Srivijaya. Meanwhile, another empire on neighboring Java was developing, called Sailendra. When they combined in the ninth century, they formed a formidable power and controlled southern Southeast Asia for 400 years.

Khmers and Thais

The main powers on mainland Southeast Asia were the Funan empire based around Cambodia, and the Chinese, who ruled over northern

Vietnam until the ninth century. Then the Khmer people arose in Cambodia to create a powerful Hindu-Buddhist empire that controlled the region for the next 300 years. The great monument of this era is Angkor, the Khmer capital city built between 900 and 1400, which includes the vast temple called Angkor Wat.

Various peoples rose up to challenge the Khmer empire, and the Thais destroyed it in 1431. The Thais then became the dominant force, with an empire based in Ayutthaya, just to the north of Bangkok.

Burma was governed by a series of Buddhist kingdoms dominated by the Mons people, including the Pagan kingdom. The city of Pagan fell into ruins after the Mongols invaded the region from the north in 1287. Today, all that

Pagan was the capital of the Kingdom of Pagan in Burma from 1044 to 1287, and was one of the most splendid cities of Southeast Asia. All the wooden buildings have rotted away, leaving just the remains of hundreds of bell-shaped Buddhist shrines called stupas.

remains of Pagan are the hundreds of *stupas*, bell-shaped monuments made of brick or stone, spread out over six square miles (16 square kilometers). It is one of Southeast Asia's most impressive historical sites.

Islam

The first European to travel extensively in the Far East was the Italian, Marco Polo. When he visited northern Sumatra in 1292, he noticed something that was to have an enormous effect on the whole of the southern part of this region: the presence of Islam. Islam, the religion of Muslims, was probably brought to the ports of northern Sumatra around 1250 by Gujerati traders from the western part of India.

Islam was founded in the seventh century by the Prophet Muhammad, who lived in Mecca, which is now in Saudi Arabia. Central to Islamic belief are the teachings of the Koran. Muslims believe that the Koran is the word of God, dictated to Muhammad by the angel Gabriel. The main principle is that there is only one god, Allah, to whom all Muslims should pray five times a day. The Koran also teaches that people should live simply, with tolerance and consideration for others. The reward for a good life is a place in heaven.

Islam, offering a simple life of devotion, was clearly attractive to Hindu Southeast Asia. Now people could succeed in life according to their merits, whereas in Hindu society they were limited by their caste. Islam spread rapidly, particularly after 1403, when it was adopted by the sultan of a new trading empire based in the port of Malacca on the Malay peninsula. From there traders took Islam up the peninsula and across to Sumatra, Java, Sulawesi, northern Borneo, and the southern Philippine islands.

By the fifteenth century, Islam was the dominant religion in the islands of Southeast Asia. In 1515 the last great Hindu empire of Java, the Majapahit, collapsed under the pressure of the new Islamic kingdoms. The royal court fled to the small neighboring island of Bali to preserve its Hindu traditions. Today, Bali is the only place in Southeast Asia where Hinduism is practiced by the majority of the inhabitants.

3   The Arrival of the Europeans

A major change took place in the late fifteenth century that was to affect the whole world. European sailors set out in small, well-armed ships to find new lands with which to trade. In particular, they wanted to find the Indies, which they thought were the source of spices.

European traders knew only that spices came from the East. They had heard something of the splendors and riches of China and India from Marco Polo, but they knew very little more than

Spices

In Roman times and in the Middle Ages spices were traded across Asia to Europe by a chain of Chinese, Indian, and Arab merchants. In Europe spices were very expensive, but in great demand.

Spices helped to preserve meat without the use of ice and also came to be used as a way of flavoring food. They were made into perfumes and were an important ingredient in medicines. The most important spices were cinnamon, cloves, nutmeg, and mace, which is found on nutmeg shells, all of which grow on trees. Ginger, a similar root called galingale, and pepper, which grows on a vine, were equally important. Cinnamon came mainly from Ceylon, but the others all grew in Southeast Asia. Cloves and nutmeg grew only in the tiny islands of the Moluccas (or Maluku) and the Banda Islands.

these tales. Clearly great fortunes could be made by any trader who could go to where these things were produced.

The Spice Islands

It was the Portuguese who pioneered the route to the real Indies. In a series of voyages they found the way around Africa to India, only to discover that the sources of the spices lay even farther east. They built a chain of forts along these routes. In 1511 a Portuguese fleet under Alfonso de Albuquerque attacked and destroyed the great trading port of Malacca. That same year Albuquerque sent an expedition farther east, and at last the main source of eastern spices was discovered. It was in the small group of islands called the Moluccas, or Maluku, and the Banda

The original port of Malacca was destroyed by the Portuguese in 1511. This Dutch print of the early 1600s shows that Malacca quickly grew into a flourishing port again, which it still is today.

Islands, at the time the only places in the world where clove and nutmeg trees were to be found.

The Philippines

The destruction of Malacca set the tone for the European entry into this region. The Portuguese had not come simply to trade in peace: they wanted to take complete control of trade. They quickly established a network of fortified ports across the region. They also felt it their duty to convert the world to Christianity. Of all the countries in Southeast Asia, however, only the Philippines became mainly Christian.

Around 1560 a Spanish commander sailed across the Pacific from Mexico and established a fort on Cebu. A series of forts was built throughout the islands, which became a Spanish

The Portuguese navigator Ferdinand Magellan first brought Christianity to the Philippines in 1521. After converting the king of Cebu, he tried to convert the people of the neighboring island of Mactan. When he and his men threatened to use force to make the people convert, they were attacked and killed. The Battle of Mactan festival is held every year on Cebu.

colony ruled from Mexico. They named it after the Spanish king of that time, Philip II.

The Spanish rulers sent Christian missionaries to the Philippines, to act as colonial officials as much as clergymen. Churches were built throughout the islands, and Spanish became the common language. The southern islands of Mindanao and Palawan, however, remained mainly Muslim.

The Dutch empire

By the end of the sixteenth century, the Dutch were set to become the greatest trading nation in the world. They were quick to see what Southeast Asia had to offer and, in 1602, founded the Dutch East India Company, soon to become Europe's biggest commercial enterprise.

The Dutch knew that the Portuguese controlled the trade to India and Europe that ran through the Strait of Malacca. They pioneered a new route to Southeast Asia that went south to the tip of Africa, then sailed due east to Java. They built their trading capital, Batavia, in 1619. Batavia is now called Jakarta.

As the Portuguese presence in Southeast Asia began to dwindle, the Dutch stepped in, taking Malacca from them in 1641. Bit by bit, they also gained control over all the islands that now make up Indonesia. Only the eastern part of the island of Timor remained Portuguese.

By the eighteenth century there were large numbers of Dutch people living in Indonesia employed as traders, officials, priests, or sailors. Many Dutchmen married local women and raised families there. These people were the first of the settlers who came to Indonesia not simply to trade and return home, but to live in the region for most of their lives. They built grand houses, banks, warehouses, roads, schools, law courts, and churches.

The Dutch and the British

Before long the British, already powerful in India, started to set up ports throughout the region. They took over the island of Penang in 1786, establishing an important foothold in Malaya. The Dutch, however, remained the most powerful nation in the region until France conquered Holland during the Napoleonic Wars in Europe, from 1799 to 1815. Britain quickly took over the Dutch possessions in Southeast Asia before France could claim them.

A young British trader and administrator, Stamford Raffles, became lieutenant governor of

The Dutch settlers became very wealthy. They built large homes and also many grand public buildings. This 1859 drawing is of a house belonging to a doctor.

Indonesia in 1811. In 1819 he founded the city of Singapore on the swampy site of the old abandoned port of Temasek, giving Britain a base at the eastern end of the Strait of Malacca. In 1824 the Dutch and the British came to an agreement whereby all islands south of the Strait of Malacca would be Dutch and anything to the north would be British. By this agreement the British now took control of Malacca.

These developments show the way events in faraway Europe came to have a direct influence on Southeast Asia. In the nineteenth century Europe's influence grew even stronger.

European might

The European nations used their wealth and power to colonize Southeast Asia. While the Dutch tightened their hold over Indonesia, the British moved into Malaya. By 1886 the British had established their rule over the entire country of Burma.

The other main European nation to enter Southeast Asia was France. After 1884 French Indochina included Vietnam, Cambodia, and Laos. Of all the Southeast Asian countries, only Thailand, called Siam at this time, was never ruled by a foreign power. Thailand, indeed, means "land of the free."

Trade and plantations

In the nineteenth century trade all over the world increased enormously, making Southeast Asia all the more important. In 1869 the Suez Canal opened, creating a route through the Mediterranean and down the Red Sea into the

Tea is grown in the cooler climate of the hills in Malaysia and Indonesia. This plantation is in the Puncak region of western Java. When ready, the young leaves at the tops of the bushes will be picked by hand.

Indian Ocean, which cut the journey from Europe to Southeast Asia by as much as a third.

The European rulers of countries such as Indonesia wanted to make them produce new goods. Tin and coal mines were developed and factories were built to process the raw materials. Above all, plantations, or massive farms, were developed to grow just one crop for export, such as tea or coffee, or tobacco or rubber.

In order to exploit this wealth still further, the colonial powers brought in thousands of laborers from India and China to work, particularly in the rubber plantations and the tin mines. They were called coolies, originally an Indian word meaning hired laborer. The intention was that they would work for a couple of years only on short-term

33

Rubber
The rubber tree, *Hevea brasiliensis,* only came to Southeast Asia in the late nineteenth century. Before this time the European nations had to import all their rubber from South America, mainly Brazil, where rubber trees grow wild. The Brazilians wanted to keep the rubber trade for themselves, but in 1876 some seeds were smuggled out and kept in Kew Gardens, London. In the 1890s, they were taken to Singapore and Malaya to start the first plantations.

Rubber had been used for some time to make erasers and waterproof clothing. The real rubber boom came in the early part of the twentieth century when large quantities of rubber were needed for tires for the first mass-produced cars.

Rubber comes from latex, a natural sap that is tapped from the trunks of the trees in the morning. The latex is mixed with acid to make rough slabs, which can then be shipped away for processing.

contracts, then return to their homeland, but many remained. In the Malay Peninsula, for instance, there were 15,000 Chinese in 1874, and two million by 1911.

The growth of resistance

The European colonial powers brought with them their own systems of government and new ideas about justice and the law, education, and medicine. The advantages of these new ideas were enjoyed by some Southeast Asians, but for most people colonial times were hard.

There was always some resistance to

colonialism, sometimes even violent uprisings. A rebellion led by Prince Diponegoro against the Dutch in Java from 1825 to 1830 cost the lives of 200,000 Javanese and 8,000 Europeans.

Not all resistance was so violent, but the colonial powers often responded harshly even to moderate pressure for change.

Asia for the Asians

Colonialism came to a sudden end in the twentieth century. It was events in the rest of the world, however, and not events in Southeast Asia, that brought this about.

In 1898 the U.S. went to war with Spain in support of the people of Cuba and gave assistance to an independence movement in the Philippines. The U.S. won the war and Spain gave the Philippines to the U.S.

The U.S. promised full independence to the Philippines, but despite this promise, progress was slow. In 1934 the Commonwealth of the Philippines was established, led by Manuel Quezon. The U.S. declared that it would give the Philippines full independence within ten years.

In 1941 the Japanese declared war by bombing the U.S. fleet in the Hawaiian port of Pearl Harbor. On the same day it also bombed Manila, the capital of the Philippines. The Europeans were totally unprepared, and the Japanese armies swept through the whole of Southeast Asia in just 122 days. Most Southeast Asians welcomed the end of European rule. They had hopes that Japan would help them to establish their own governments because the Japanese slogan was "Asia for the Asians."

4 The Struggle for Independence

As it turned out, the Japanese were no kinder to the Southeast Asians than were their old colonial masters. Many people were cruelly treated. The Japanese especially hated the Chinese.

When the U.S. dropped atomic bombs on the Japanese cities of Hiroshima and Nagasaki in 1945, the Japanese surrendered and the war came to an end. The British, Dutch, and French thought that they would now be able to come back to Southeast Asia and resume their domination. However, after four years of Japanese occupation, the Southeast Asian nations wanted independence, and they were prepared to fight for it.

The first tastes of independence

During World War II, the Filipinos fought heroically against the Japanese, assisting the Americans to bring about a victory. One million Filipinos are believed to have died and Manila was devastated. The U.S. was quick to honor its promises. In 1946 the Philippines were granted full independence. As a concession, the U.S. was allowed to keep two huge military bases on the islands.

Burma had also been the scene of grueling fighting during the war, where British troops had adopted the tactics of jungle warfare to prevent the Japanese from invading India. Burma was given independence by the British in 1948.

The Dutch in Indonesia

Indonesia was the scene of the most bitter struggles immediately after the war. When the Japanese left, they handed over power to Ahmed Sukarno who then declared independence and vowed to resist Dutch attempts to regain power.

After violent actions against Sukarno's republican forces caused great horror in the rest of the world, the Dutch were forced to hold talks with the Indonesians in 1949. All the Indonesian islands once ruled by the Dutch, except West Irian, then became the independent Republic of Indonesia, with Sukarno as its first president. West Irian became a part of Indonesia in 1963.

The Malayan "Emergency"

The British had a smoother path when they returned to Malaya. In 1945 it became a crown colony composed of a federation of the various states of the Malay Peninsula.

In 1948, however, pressure for complete independence erupted in violence. Throughout the war Communist groups, formed mainly by the Chinese and often helped by the British, had fought against the Japanese. Now these groups attempted to take over the government of Malaya, triggering what is known as "the Emergency."

The British realized that they would never be able to hold on to power, and in 1957 Malaya became independent. The new Federation of Malaya consisted of the nine sultanates of peninsular Malaya and the Straits Settlements of Penang and Malacca. The British handed over power to the ruling assemblies of the states.

In 1963 Singapore and the northern Borneo states of Sarawak and Sabah joined Malaya, creating the Federation of Malaysia. In 1965, however, Singapore withdrew and became completely independent. This move was made primarily because Singapore felt that the Malays were being allowed to dominate Malaysia at the expense of the Chinese. Seventy-five percent of the people of Singapore are Chinese.

The Vietnam War
Vietnam had been ruled by the French since the second half of the nineteenth century. During World War II, a group of Communists and Nationalists led by Ho Chi Minh fought for independence against the Japanese. After the war they continued to fight against the French for eight years. In 1954 France was completely defeated at the battle of Dien Bien Phu, and withdrew from Vietnam.

At this point, by international agreement, Vietnam was divided in two while awaiting open elections. North Vietnam was ruled by the Communists and South Vietnam was ruled by the Nationalists. Before the elections could take place, however, the Nationalists declared South Vietnam to be an independent republic. Communists in South Vietnam (called Viet Cong), heavily supported by North Vietnam, began a war with the intention of removing the South Vietnamese government. The South Vietnamese government gained the support of the U.S.

It was not until 1965, however, that the U.S. began to commit its own soldiers to battle, and

These guns, boots, and helmets have been erected as a battlefield memorial to some of the 57,000 U.S. soldiers who died in the Vietnam War. The U.S. became involved when it backed the South Vietnamese government against the Communist Viet Cong, who were supported by North Vietnam.

then the war escalated quickly. Although the U.S. had far better weapons and equipment, they found it impossible to hunt down the Viet Cong. Two million Vietnamese people died, many of them women and children. The Vietnam War also cost the American people enormous sums of money, and the lives of 57,000 of their young men. The war also spilled over into Laos and Cambodia.

By 1973 the war had become enormously unpopular in the U.S. When Americans realized

Vietnam and the "Boat People"
Since 1978 hundreds of thousands of Vietnamese have risked their lives to flee their country, often crammed into tiny, rickety fishing boats. At first the so-called "boat people" were from South Vietnam, fleeing from harsh treatment by the victorious North Vietnamese. Later they came also from North Vietnam, driven away by poverty and by the lack of any signs of improvement. Some 1.5 million Vietnamese have now left their country and have found homes abroad. Others have managed to escape, only to be held in camps in neighboring countries: 80,000 in Thailand and 57,000 in Hong Kong. There seems to be no solution to the problem until the economy of Vietnam improves, which may only happen if it receives international aid from more prosperous countries. At present it only receives help from the Soviet Union and eastern European nations, in exchange for raw materials. In theory Vietnam has the resources to become one of the richest countries in the region.

that they could not win, they began pulling their troops out. In 1975 Saigon, the old capital of South Vietnam, fell to the North Vietnamese, and Vietnam was united as one country under a Communist government based in North Vietnam's capital Hanoi. Saigon's name was changed to Ho Chi Minh City.

Cambodia
Cambodia won its independence from France in 1953 and was ruled in comparative peace and prosperity by Prince Sihanouk until 1970.

When the Americans bombed Cambodia, hundreds of thousands of Cambodians fled to the capital, Phnom Penh. Prince Sihanouk was removed from power by an army general called Lon Nol, with the support of the U.S. At the same time Communists in Cambodia, called the Khmer Rouge, started fighting against Lon Nol's government.

In 1975, after the U.S. had withdrawn from Southeast Asia, the Khmer Rouge forced their way into Phnom Penh and took control of the government. For the next three years Cambodia was subjected to one of the most terrifying nightmares of modern history. The Khmer Rouge, led by Pol Pot, wanted to create an entirely new society. To achieve this they set about wiping out all signs of traditional or western society. They believed that only peasants working on the land could bring about this new society. So all the towns were emptied of people, and everyone had to work in the fields in virtual slavery. The Khmer Rouge killed all the doctors, teachers, engineers—indeed anyone who had been educated. Despite the fact that this was once a leading rice-producing nation, the farming experiment was a disaster and thousands died of famine. In just three years about two million Cambodians died through starvation, disease, or murder—almost 33 percent of the total population. The majority of the dead were men, so now there are only three men to every seven women.

In December 1978 the Vietnamese invaded Cambodia because of attacks by the Khmer Rouge along its western border. They drove the Khmer

Rouge out, forcing them over the border into Thailand. Only then was the world aware of the horror that the Cambodian nation had suffered.

The Vietnamese remained in Cambodia for ten years before withdrawing their troops in 1989. Meanwhile the Khmer Rouge formed an alliance with other groups opposed to Vietnamese occupation, including the supporters of Prince Sihanouk. From their refugee camps in Thailand they were able to attack border towns inside Cambodia, threatening to plunge the nation into civil war again. China continued to support the Khmer Rouge by supplying arms.

In this confused situation Cambodia received almost no help from the outside world. It has been quite unable to revive its economy and remains poor and underdeveloped.

Other regional agonies

In the 1960s President Sukarno's Indonesia began to run into serious economic difficulties. Inflation was running at 100 percent; in other words, prices were doubling every year. There was widespread corruption as government officials and army officers took bribes in return for special favors. Sukarno started a disastrous war with Malaya in order to try to disrupt the creation of the Federation of Malaysia. Meanwhile the Communist party was growing in strength. In 1965 a group of senior army officers was killed in a coup, which is an attempt to seize power by force. The Communists were blamed and a bloodbath followed, claiming the lives of some 500,000 people. This spelled the end of President Sukarno and he was soon replaced by Suharto. Under

President Corazón Aquino receiving gifts of traditional cakes from the women of Samar, the Philippine's poorest island. This trip in January 1988 was her first official trip outside Manila after an attempted coup in December 1987.

President Suharto, Indonesia has found a new stability and has prospered.

The Philippines was ruled from 1965 to 1986 by President Ferdinand Marcos. At first, he was welcomed as a genuine "man of the people" and had widespread public support. In 1972, however, a crisis was caused by the threat of civil war from Communist guerrillas. President Marcos declared martial law, which gave him enormous power. There was widespread repression, imprisonment, and torture. Soon it was clear that Marcos and his friends were becoming increasingly rich, while the rest of the nation became poorer. In 1986 Marcos was removed from office by popular vote. He was

43

replaced by Corazón Aquino, the widow of Benigno Aquino, an opposition leader who had been murdered in 1983 at the Manila airport by supporters of President Marcos.

Under President Aquino, the economy of the Philippines has grown by an impressive six percent a year. The country, however, is still troubled. The army has attempted to seize power half a dozen times. Communist and Muslim guerrillas are still active on a number of islands. Most Filipinos remain very poor and many have had to leave their homeland to find work abroad.

The closed nations

Two nations of Indochina have turned their backs on the outside world since independence. These two countries are Burma and Laos. They remain

These people in the Burmese capital, Rangoon, have been cut off from events outside Burma since 1974 when the military socialist government took command. Since then, no new developments have been allowed and most places look very run down.

among the poorest nations in the world.

When the French left Laos in 1954, the Communist Pathet Lao party ruled the eastern part. The western part, with the capital Vientiane, or Viangchan, was ruled by the king, with American support. In 1975 the Pathet Lao took over the whole country. Since then Laos has remained a quiet land, living mainly from its modest agriculture, always suffering from the fact that it is landlocked.

Burma has been ruled by the army since 1962. In 1974 the military government declared itself to be the Burma Socialist Program party. It decided that the country would be socialist, with an economy run for the benefit of the people; that it would be Buddhist; and that it would close itself off completely from the outside world. As a result, Burma has remained stuck in the past. In recent years there have been riots led by students and Buddhists that have been harshly put down by the military government.

Meanwhile large sections of the country are in a state of war. Burma is ruled by the Burmans, who make up 65 percent of the population and occupy the central plains. In the mountains around the plains live various other groups of people, in particular the Karens, the Shans, and the Kachins, who do not wish to be ruled by the Burmans. These groups all want independence, and they have some 20,000 soldiers who are fighting a guerrilla war to achieve it.

ASEAN
Burma, Laos, Cambodia, and Vietnam remain some of the poorest countries in the world. Other

countries in Southeast Asia, however, have begun to prosper in recent decades.

Prosperity is linked to political stability. The countries that have had peace and a stable government have been able to devote their energies to developing their economies. An important element in this political stability has been the creation of ASEAN, the Association of Southeast Asian Nations. This was formed in 1967 and there are six member-countries: Indonesia, Malaysia, Thailand, Singapore, the Philippines, and Brunei.

The aim of ASEAN is to create a framework of cooperation through which Southeast Asian nations can discuss and solve regional problems. It has been highly successful in giving Southeast Asia an identity of its own. Its growing importance has also coincided with the rapid economic development of most of the member countries.

5   The Business Boom

The Southeast Asian nations have had to confront the enormous difficulties that they inherited from their colonial past. The European nations mainly wanted raw materials from their colonies. They could trade these profitably on the world market because they were cheap, and they were cheap because the workers in the mines and plantations were paid very low wages.

After the war, these newly independent countries no longer had the guaranteed markets for their produce that the colonial system enjoyed. They found that they would now have to sell their produce in competition with the rest of the world. Furthermore, the world had moved away from heavy industry. Wealth was no longer to be found in producing only raw materials.

The successful countries of Southeast Asia realized this fact. They set about creating new industries and modernizing their agricultural systems in order to produce the goods that the rest of the world would want to buy. These countries, particularly Singapore, Thailand, Malaysia, and Indonesia, have set the pace. They have given the region as a whole one of the fastest-growing economies in the world.

The new industries

Southeast Asia's first successes in modern industry arose from two main factors. First, Southeast Asia has a skilled workforce, able to learn new techniques and able to produce complex, high-quality goods. Second, the cost of living is comparatively cheap, so wages are low.

The result of these advantages is that Southeast Asia can produce high-quality goods at low prices. Electrical goods such as televisions, radios, and food processors are manufactured in small factories, where semiskilled workers operate machinery on a production line. Other factories make clothing, shoes, watches, and toys, while there are larger industrial plants producing chemicals and fertilizer. High-tech industries producing advanced electrical goods and computer components have been developed in Malaysia, Thailand, and especially in Singapore, while the Philippines is the world's largest producer of computer microchips.

Many of these industries have been set up by the local branches of major international

Southeast Asia has developed a strong electronics industry. This microchip factory is in Penang, Malaysia.

48

companies based in Japan, Europe, or the U.S. The prosperous Southeast Asian nations have tended to encourage this kind of investment. It means that the overseas company has to meet the expenses of building the factories and getting the business going. It also brings employment and valuable work experience to local people. The danger of such investment is that all profits may go to the company abroad. Most Southeast Asian countries have been careful to negotiate special deals with international companies to ensure that they evenly share the profits.

Modernized agriculture

The vast majority of people in Southeast Asia still live off the land. With so many mouths to feed, and with populations growing all the time, it is essential for these developing nations to have efficient agricultural systems so that they can feed themselves and do not have to import food. Science has played an increasing role in improving agriculture.

Rice is by far the most important food in the region. Over the last 20 years, rice production has grown enormously throughout the region. In the so-called Green Revolution a new strain of rice known as "miracle rice" began to be widely used. This rice gives high yields and grows quickly enough to produce three harvests a year, whereas traditional strains of rice produce just two. Rice is now produced in such quantities that much of it is exported. Indonesia is now the third largest producer of rice in the world, Thailand the fifth.

The plantations still play an important part in the economy of the region. Tea and coffee are grown in the cooler hills of Malaysia and Java; sugarcane in the Philippines, Thailand, and Indonesia. There are coconut plantations throughout the region, chiefly for the production of coconut oil. Spices are still grown for export, especially cloves, nutmeg, and pepper. Indonesia itself consumes large quantities of cloves because most of its cigarettes are flavored with crushed cloves.

Rubber used to be Malaysia's main export product, but rubber is now being increasingly replaced by synthetic products. As a result Malaysia has begun to switch from rubber to oil palms. It now produces 80 percent of the world's palm oil, which is used to make margarine, soap, and candles.

Fish-farming, by which fish are raised in controlled conditions in tanks, has become a

An abundant supply of a variety of woods has made woodcarving one of the many traditional skills that have been developed to boost the income of Southeast Asian countries. These young woodcarvers are in a workshop in Thailand.

major industry, especially in Singapore, the Philippines, and Thailand. Other important agricultural products include corn, cassava (which is made into tapioca), coffee, and jute.

Timber
There is a huge demand for tropical hardwoods such as teak, mahogany, and ebony. Industrialized countries are prepared to pay high prices for these woods. Southeast Asia supplies the world with 70 percent of its hardwoods. Meanwhile great quantities of the region's less valuable timber are made into plywood.

At the beginning of this century there were some 1 million square miles (2.5 million square kilometers) of forest in Southeast Asia. Barely a quarter of this now remains. The speed with which the logging industry is consuming the forests is now causing widespread concern. It is estimated that at the present rate all the tropical rain forest of Southeast Asia will disappear within 30 years. Deforestation recently caused a disastrous series of floods in southern Thailand. In Borneo, remote tribes and rare animals are threatened with extinction as ever larger areas of forest are cleared by bulldozers and chainsaws.

Hardwood forests have to be carefully managed. By limiting the amount of trees cut down each year, it is possible to provide a supply of timber without destroying the forests. Indonesia is making efforts to do this and now claims to have 7.5 million acres (3 million hectares) of managed hardwood forests. In 1985 it stopped exporting raw timber. Meanwhile, in 1989, Thailand announced that it would stop

The worldwide demand for timber has led to the destruction of 75 percent of the tropical forest in Southeast Asia. There are now some attempts to control the cutting of timber to avoid the total devastation seen here in Malaysia.

logging altogether, although it would continue to import wood from Burma and Laos. It remains to be seen whether these measures will be enough to save the forests and timber industry.

Mineral wealth

One of the attractions of foreign traders to Southeast Asia has always been its wealth of minerals. There is copper in Indonesia and the Philippines, gold in the Philippines, and coal in Vietnam. Malaysia has supplies of coal, iron ore, bauxite, gold, and manganese. Over 50 percent of the world's tin comes from this region, and it is found in large quantities in Malaysia, Indonesia, and Burma. Most of the world's rubies and sapphires come from Burma and Thailand.

Tin is one of the many minerals found in Malaysia. It is extracted by using water and dredgers, which is very damaging to the landscape. The Malaysian Peninsula produces over 30,000 tons of tin a year.

All these are, however, less important than petroleum, which is extremely valuable. The main petroleum-producing countries of Southeast Asia are Indonesia and Brunei, but oil is also found in Malaysia, Thailand, Vietnam, and Burma. Much of the oil is drilled offshore on oil rigs suspended over the sea. The oil is often found in conjunction with natural gas, which is used widely in industry. Indonesia is now the world's largest exporter of liquefied natural gas, LNG, sending it mainly to Japan and South Korea.

Tourism

Over the last 20 or 30 years tourism has become a major industry in Southeast Asia. The region has a great deal to offer tourists. It has beautiful beaches and a warm, sunny climate. It has magnificent ancient monuments, such as Pagan in Burma and Borobodur in Java. It has excellent, spicy food. It has a rich and varied culture that can offer music, dance, colorful festivals, and spectacular religious ceremonies. For the more adventurous, there are uncharted regions of thick forest where travelers can see a wide range of wildlife and visit the villages of remote tribes.

There are some superbly designed hotels in the main tourist resorts of Malaysia, Singapore, Thailand, Indonesia, and the Philippines. These hotels often combine traditional styles with the most modern materials.

Southeast Asia is one of the world's most exciting regions for tourists, millions of whom arrive every year from Europe, the U.S., and

One of the many tourist attractions in Southeast Asia is the temple complex at Wat Phrahat near Chiang Mai, Thailand. This huge mythical serpent bordering the long stairway to the temples is called a naga.

Japan. The tourist industry brings in a great deal of foreign money. Hundreds of thousands of people are employed as hotel staff, drivers, tour operators, and guides. Many more people benefit by being able to sell crafts and souvenirs, drinks and postcards to tourists.

Tourism is not always a blessing, however. Tourists, with their great wealth and their foreign ways, can often harm the delicate balances that exist in traditional societies. It is for this reason that Burma has restricted all tourists to a visit of seven days only. Tourists are not welcomed at all in Brunei. Few tourists visit Cambodia, Laos, and Vietnam because of the difficulties of traveling there since the end of the Vietnam War.

The benefits of the modern world

Prosperity can be used in two ways: it can be used to improve the standard of living of everyone, or it can be used to make just a few people very wealthy. Both of these processes are at work in Southeast Asia.

The most prosperous nations have chosen a middle course between the two. In Malaysia, Singapore, Thailand, and Indonesia, some people are extremely wealthy, while most people live modestly. Standards of living, however, are improving in a number of ways. There are better roads and systems of public transportation, better supplies of electricity and clean water, improved medical care, and better schools. Successful businesses, especially tourism, depend upon good transportation systems, by road, rail, air, and sea. They also need efficient banks and telephone systems. As businesses insist on improvements in these aspects of daily life, ordinary people also benefit.

The cities are usually the first places to show signs of new prosperity. Impressive modern office buildings, with stylish entrance halls and elevators, air-conditioning, even swimming pools and gyms, are being built increasingly in Bangkok, Kuala Lumpur, Jakarta, and Manila. These developments often seem to follow the style of life set by the cities of Europe and the U.S. Alongside the shining new office buildings are American-style fast-food restaurants, supermarkets and department stores, discotheques and fashionable clothes stores.

In the major cities of Southeast Asia, traditional housing lies alongside thriving commercial areas, as here in Jakarta, the capital of Indonesia. The old housing areas are often very poor and overcrowded.

The cities are not paved with gold

The riches of the big cities act like a magnet to

56

young people who are brought up in the much poorer villages of the surrounding countryside. Every year thousands leave their homes and head for the cities, hoping to find work and make their fortunes. Most of them will be disappointed.

The cities highlight the most striking and cruel contrasts between rich and poor. Within a short distance of the modern city centers are the traditional quarters, thronged with people and traffic. The streets are filled with bicycles, battered cars, and mini-taxis converted from scooters, belching out fumes and honking their horns. Trays of fruits and vegetables, dried fish, cigarettes, ballpoint pens, and mosquito spray from the tiny stores lining the street spill out over the pavements. Street vendors push their carts down the road, selling brightly colored soft drinks and hot dishes such as noodles or fried chicken. There are miniature restaurants tucked among the stores, with tables covered wtih plastic cloths and simple wooden benches. Above them are cramped apartments, shutters flung open so the humid tropical air can circulate. Laundry hangs from the balconies and dusty potted plants sit on the windowsills. Families of ten or more may live in three rooms. They are the lucky ones.

Out on the edges of the cities are the shantytowns. Here the poorer families live in tumbledown wooden shacks on unwanted land, often by the edge of stagnant and polluted rivers or directly under the flight path of an airport. These people do menial, backbreaking jobs, ferrying people about in bicycle-driven "pedicabs" selling newspapers and cigarettes at the bus stations. There is real poverty in such

Many poor families live in homes that are only tumbledown shacks. They are often beside rivers heavily polluted by sewage and other waste. This results in widespread disease.

districts and it will take many years for prosperity to reach these people.

Singapore

Singapore is the only major city in Southeast Asia where such poverty is less prevalent. Since independence in 1965, Singapore has developed rapidly into one of the world's most advanced and successful nations.

Singapore consists of one main island and 57 smaller ones. The total land area is just 220 square miles (570 square kilometers). Some 2.5 million people live here, 75 percent of whom are Chinese. The remainder are mainly Malay (15 percent) and Indian (7 percent). A small amount of land is reserved for intensive farming, but about 80

Singapore is one of the most thriving and dynamic cities in the world. It is an important center for banking as well as having a variety of industries. It is a very crowded city; there are about 11,000 people per square mile (4,000 per square kilometer).

percent of Singapore's food has to be imported. How can such a tiny nation survive? The answer lies in the exceptional energy of its people. Singapore has developed into a leading producer of electrical equipment, computers, textiles, and clothing. It is the region's most important financial center with banks, insurance services, and a stock exchange. It has the world's second largest port, serving some 60,000 ships from all over the world every year. Singapore is also a busy tourist center, with about three million tourists a year.

Singapore is one of the world's most modern cities, with some very impressive architecture. Satellite telecommunications connect the city to all other parts of the world. A new and efficient underground railroad system transports people

within the city. There is also a busy modern airport serving 49 of the world's leading airlines, including its own airline, Singapore Airways.

Some 85 percent of Singaporeans live in modern apartment buildings built and owned by the government. Schools are good and the hospitals are the best in Southeast Asia.

Many of Singapore's laws seem strict to outsiders. Newspapers and television are controlled by the government, which does not welcome criticism. Singaporeans' ability to accept these restrictions as discipline has played a major part in the success of their nation.

The Chinese in Southeast Asia

The Chinese have been present in Southeast Asia since the beginning of history. At first they came as traders, not as conquerors, although they ruled over northern Vietnam for many centuries. In the nineteenth century, thousands came as hired laborers to work in the mines and plantations.

The Chinese are noted for being excellent at business. Where they settled in the ports and cities, they became the shopkeepers and the moneylenders. They often led their lives apart from the rest of the community. The major cities had "Chinatowns" where the Chinese communities lived, spoke their own language, and maintained their traditional ways.

This has given rise to a curious situation. On the one hand, many of the most successful businesses of Southeast Asia are run by the Chinese. At the same time, the Chinese are distrusted and their success is often deeply resented. In many Southeast Asian countries they are shunned and do not enjoy the same rights as their fellow citizens.

---

6   Traditional Ways

Throughout Southeast Asia you will see signs of the modern world, from the brand-new office buildings in the cities to radios and motorbikes in a remote village. In cities and small towns you will find people wearing jeans and T-shirts, listening to American and European pop music, and traveling in Japanese minibuses.

Nonetheless the Southeast Asian way of life remains very traditional in many ways. About 75 percent of the people live in small villages in the countryside, and in remote areas village life goes on virtually unchanged, as it has done for centuries. Families live in simple houses. People have little money, but they have shelter, clothing,

The traditional dress of Southeast Asia for men and women is the sarong, a simple wraparound skirt made of a single large rectangle of cloth. These Balinese women, attending a cremation ceremony, are also wearing the typical tight-fitting jacket known as a kebaya.

61

and enough food to lead a dignified life. Even in the cities there are all kinds of reminders of old traditions, from the temples and mosques to the food people eat and the clothes that they wear.

Temples, mosques, and churches
Religion plays an important part in the lives of most Southeast Asians. The region can be divided into three principal religious blocks. Mainland Southeast Asia is mainly Buddhist, Indonesia and Malaysia are mainly Muslim, and the Philippines are mainly Christian.

The religious map of Southeast Asia is not quite as simple as this, however. There are Christians living in Indonesia and Vietnam. There are Muslims in the southern Philippines and in southern Thailand. The island of Bali in Indonesia is almost totally Hindu, and there are Hindus of Indian origin in Singapore and Malaysia. The Chinese follow their own traditions, mixing the ancient philosophies of Confucianism and Taoism with even more ancient traditions of ancestor worship.

Religions are practiced actively throughout the region. It is fairly common to see a new temple being built in Thailand. The builders use modern materials such as concrete and steel, decorated with glittering pieces of colored glass. There are numerous new and impressive mosques in Malaysia and Indonesia. In the Philippines the colorful little buses called "jeepneys" almost always include a picture of Christ or the saints and a written prayer in their lavish and gaudy decorations. Even in Laos and Vietnam, where the Communist rulers disapprove of any form of religion, Buddhism and Christianity have survived.

The greatest Muslim population in the world

Islam is the most prevalent religion of Southeast Asia. There are 160 million Muslims in Indonesia alone, making this by far the world's largest Muslim country. Throughout the Muslim parts of Southeast Asia you will see large and small mosques, with their glinting metallic domes and spindly towers called minarets. Each day begins with the call to prayer, chanted in Arabic by the *muezzin* in the mosque and broadcast on loudspeakers across the towns and villages. This call to prayer is repeated five times a day, making it a familiar sound in the region.

Malaysia and Brunei are also mostly Muslim.

The majority of the population of the oil-rich island of Brunei is Muslim. Large amounts of money have been spent on magnificent mosques, such as the Omar Ali Saifuddin mosque in Bandar Seri Begawan, the capital.

The Distribution of Religions in Southeast Asia

Country	Principal religions
Indonesia	Muslim (88%), Christian, Hindu
Brunei	Muslim (62%), Buddhist, Christian
Malaysia	Muslim (50%), Buddhist (26%), Hindu, Christian, Taoist, Confucianist
Burma	Buddhist (95%)
Thailand	Buddhist (95%), Muslim
Cambodia	Buddhist (90%), Muslim, Christian
Laos	Buddhist (58%)
Vietnam	Buddhist (58%), Christian
Philippines	Christian (92%), Muslim
Singapore	Buddhist, Muslim, Hindu, Christian, Taoist, Confucianist

Both of these countries are Islamic states, whose laws are based on the laws of Islam, as described in the holy book, the Koran. Indonesia, however, is not an Islamic state. Under its constitution all religions are tolerated, provided that they have only one god.

By and large, Islam in Southeast Asia is a gentle religion, and not as strict and severe as it is in some Middle Eastern countries. There are, however, many Muslims who would like to see everyone obey Islamic traditions more strictly. Increasingly in Indonesia, for example, Muslim girls have to cover their heads with scarves or veils when they attend school.

A home in the tropics
For most people in Southeast Asia, home is a simple house built of materials that grow locally—

wood or bamboo, with a thatch of palm fronds. This is quite enough for this warm climate. In rural areas, even the houses of the wealthy only differ from the poorer houses in their size and in the quality of the workmanship. Wealthier homes may have carved wooden doors, polished floors, and neatly fitting shutters.

Inside these houses there is very little furniture. Families sleep on thin mattresses rolled out on the wooden floor. There is almost no privacy. The kitchen may be just a shed at the back of the house where the cooking is done over an open fire of coconut husks. When the family comes together to eat, they collect around the kitchen in informal groups, sit on the steps of the house, or stand.

The houses may be simple, but they are

Villages in the hills and mountains may be very simple indeed, such as this one to the north of Chiang Mai in Thailand. The houses are built on stilts to protect them from the monsoon rains. The roofs are made out of traditional grass thatch.

generally kept clean and well swept. They must also be strong enough to keep out the heavy monsoon rains. Houses are often built on stilts for this reason. In some places, houses are built over water. An area of Bangkok known as the *klongs* is built over a large expanse of land that is permanently flooded by the Chao Phraya River. Boats are used instead of cars to ferry people to work or to the stores.

Of course, each village is different. Increasingly these days, manufactured building materials are used, even in poor villages. Floors may be made of concrete. The roof may be made of corrugated iron or tiles. Windows may be fitted with panes of glass. Certainly, these houses are stronger and last longer, but they are often less comfortable to live in when the weather is hot. The old style of house remains popular.

Villages and families

In most villages throughout Southeast Asia there is a strong sense of community. Usually, a village will consist of a number of very large families. Every house is likely to be the home of not only a married couple and their children, but grandparents, aunts and uncles, and nieces and nephews. The village is run by a council of villagers, usually the married men. They appoint a headman who presides over their meetings and acts as a kind of mayor.

Village meetings are called regularly to discuss all matters concerning the community. Everyone has a say in the decisions made. The result is that villages tend to be harmonious places, which give their inhabitants a strong sense of belonging.

There are a number of groups of people in Southeast Asia who are called "sea-gypsies." They live in villages that are built on stilts over the sea in shallow water. Their main occupation is fishing. Despite the precarious look of these villages, they are often just as sophisticated as similar villages on dry land.

Even when people leave their village and go to the cities, they will return regularly to keep in touch with their families and to attend weddings, religious festivals, and other special occasions. The Vietnamese have an expression for this: "Leaves always fall back to the roots of the tree."

Many Southeast Asian cities are really just a mass of villages that have grown together. In Indonesia, for example, the rural villages are known as *kampungs*, but the cities are also divided into kampungs. Community life in these city kampungs has very much the same kind of structure as in the small kampungs in the countryside.

Market day
In all rural areas there are regular markets where

67

villagers come to sell their surplus products. Traders also come to the markets, selling clothes, shoes, tools, kitchen utensils, spices, and dried fish. Markets provide an opportunity for villagers to earn a little money and buy the things that they cannot produce or make themselves. It is also a time for them to get together and chat and enjoy themselves. For the visitor from abroad, markets are one of the great spectacles of Southeast Asia, full of color and exotic sights and smells.

Rice

The rural villages depend on farming for their livelihood, and just as the houses are simple and traditional, so are the methods of agriculture. Rice is the most important crop. This is primarily "wet rice," which grows in flooded paddy fields (from the Malay word *padi*, meaning "rice growing in the field"). Where water is scarce,

---

Coconuts

Coconut palms are found everywhere in Southeast Asia. They are exceptionally useful trees. The white flesh of the coconut is grated and made into coconut "milk," widely used for flavoring food. The juice of young coconuts is rich and pure and makes a refreshing drink, and the jelly lining the husk of young coconuts is used to feed babies. Copra, the dried white flesh of mature coconuts, is used to make coconut oil, the most common cooking oil of the region. Coconuts come in thick, fibrous husks, which are burned as fuel. The palm fronds are used as roofing and for making matting and baskets, and the wood is used as timber, to make beams for houses.

"dry rice" is grown in unflooded fields.

The edges of the paddy fields have to be carefully banked up to hold in the water. They are often built as a series of steps, following the contours of the hills and valleys—a spectacular sight. Some of the most impressive rice terraces are believed to be 3,000 years old. Complicated irrigation systems feed water from the springs and rivers to the paddy fields. This requires a great deal of cooperation between farmers.

Betelnut

In any rural area in Southeast Asia you might see someone suddenly spit a jet of bright red fluid onto the ground. This can be an alarming sight because it looks just like blood. In fact, it is the juice of betelnut, which many people chew as a habit, just as others smoke cigarettes. Betelnut is the seed of the areca palm. It is said to help digestion and is mildly intoxicating. Many old people's teeth are stained black and red from years of chewing betelnut. The habit is less popular with younger people than it has been in the past.

These women in a village market near Pagan, Burma, are selling betel leaves. These are combined with betelnut, which is popular for chewing throughout Southeast Asia. Behind the women, chilies are displayed for sale.

"Eat rice"

"Staple" is used to describe any food that is the central, most important food in a region. In Southeast Asia, rice is so much the staple food that the term "to eat rice" is the same as saying "to eat" in some languages. Rice is eaten as much as three times a day by the vast majority of people. It is accompanied by a variety of sauces, usually consisting of vegetables with perhaps a scrap of chicken or dried fish and plenty of peppers to make it spicy-hot.

On a market day, or in any idle moment in town, a quick snack may be irresistible. Snacks are sold in tiny market stands or from large carts that are pushed along the streets. Noodles are a great favorite, fried with fresh vegetables in the Chinese way in piping hot oil. On feast days, Southeast Asians show their love of good food. Southeast Asia, and particularly Thailand, has some of the most delicious food in the world. Famous dishes from Thailand include *dom yam gung,* a soup of prawns cooked in chicken stock flavored with lemon grass, spring onions, and chopped hot peppers. There are dishes of fresh fish dusted with crushed spices and steamed in an envelope of banana leaves. Delicious curries, borrowed originally from India, are cooked in coconut milk. Malaysia is famous for its *satay,* small kebabs of chicken or goat that have been coated in a thick sauce of ground peanuts, grated coconut, spices, and peppers and cooked over a charcoal fire. *Gado-gado* uses a similar peanut sauce spread over lightly steamed vegetables and served with crispy, featherlike crackers made of cassava flour. Philippine cooking is a succulent mixture of Southeast Asian spices and coconut, with Spanish elements such as tomatoes and sausages.

Southeast Asians do not generally eat desserts, but they may end a meal with a piece of fresh fruit. There are numerous delicious fruits to choose from, ranging from bananas, oranges, apples, and grapes to less familiar tropical fruits such as rambutans, guavas, papayas, mangoes, and the grapefruitlike pomelo.

People do not really drink or eat milk and milk products. Milk, yogurt, and cheese might be found in the cities, but not in the villages.

Unique traditions
Many parts of Southeast Asia have their own quite distinct peoples or tribes. These people follow their own traditions in their villages, with their own religions and their own languages. Often, they do not even speak the language of the country in which they live, and consider themselves to be more or less independent.

There are a number of such groups in northern Thailand and Burma. The Akha people, for example, come originally from southern China. They move across the borders in the mountains and set up villages in territory that they claim as theirs. Akha women wear distinctive headdresses of black and red cloth decorated with a mass of beads and silver discs and rings, quite different from any other Thai costume. In northern Borneo the Iban people live in longhouses. Whole villages will live in one huge, longhouse, made entirely of wood and built on stilts. The Toraja of Sulawesi also have distinctive houses, beautifully decorated wooden structures with great curving roofs. The Toraja are famous for the way they treat their dead. At funerals, huge numbers of pigs and buffaloes are slaughtered, before the body of the dead person is laid to rest in a hole in the cliffs. The spirits of the dead are represented by lifelike wooden statues, which are carefully dressed in good clothes and placed near the grave.

Untouched by the modern world

The Akha people of northern Thailand were originally from China. They still have their own style of costume and their own language.

There are other people living in Southeast Asia who lead lives that have barely changed in thousands of years. These people live in such remote parts of the region that they were not affected by the arrival of Hinduism, or Buddhism, or Islam, or even the colonial powers.

There are many tribes in Southeast Asia whose lives have been barely touched by the outside world. On the island of Sarawak, this Land Dayak girl carries water from the river in bamboo tubes. Her tribe still lives by hunting and collecting food from the jungle.

The Penan people live in the Mulu forest in Borneo. They are nomads, moving from place to place in search of food. Their staple food is a dough made from the inner pith of the wild sago palm. They also eat deer, turtles, frogs, wild honey, insects, and fungi.

It is said that the Penan people have been living this way for 40,000 years. However, the way of life of all such remote tribes is under threat. Gradually the forests are being stripped for their valuable woods. When the modern world reaches these areas it often brings its diseases, against which the people have no natural resistance. Even 20 years ago there were far more of these remote peoples than there are today.

73

7 Authority and Care

Village life and traditional ways have given the Southeast Asian nations a solid base from which to face the many changes of recent decades. A number of very strong leaders have made their mark on the recent history of the region: Lee Kuan Yew, the prime minister of Singapore, for example; Mahathir Mohamad, the prime minister of Malaysia; Sukarno and Suharto, presidents of Indonesia; Ferdinand Marcos and Corazón Aquino, presidents of the Philippines.

In return, successful leaders have to stay in line with the wishes of the people. There is a Malay tradition called *musyawarah*. This translates as "consensus," the agreement of the majority in every decision. The tradition is said to owe its origin to rice farming, which depends on very complex systems of irrigation; to work properly each decision has to have the agreement of all the participants. According to this tradition the best kind of government is achieved when all problems are discussed fully in order to find the solution that takes into account everyone's wishes. It is, of course, not always possible to do so. Nevertheless, this is the ideal against which much of Southeast Asian politics is judged.

The political mosaic
The Southeast Asian nations now evidence a variety of types of government, ranging from Communist one-party states to monarchies. The Philippines has a democratically elected

government led by a president, similar to the American system. Indonesia is ruled by a powerful president who chooses his own cabinet of ministers; laws are passed by a large elected assembly. Thailand is a monarchy with an elected government that maintains close ties with the army. The head of state is the king, who retains certain powers under the constitution. Singapore has an elected parliament and a powerful president. The People's Action party dominates the elections to such an extent that in the 1988 election only one seat was won by an opposition party. Brunei is ruled by the sultan, who appoints his own cabinet. Burma is ruled by a group of unelected army officers kept in power by the strength of the armed forces.

Malaysia has its own complex and rather unusual system of government. Each of the 13 states has an elected assembly, with a chief minister who represents the party with the most members in the assembly. There is also a national parliament consisting of an elected House of Representatives, and a Senate, half of which is elected and half of which is appointed by the prime minister. The prime minister is the leader of the party with the most representatives in parliament. There is also a king, one of the nine sultans of Malaysia, who is the head of state. The king serves a five-year term, then the nine sultans convene to elect a new king.

Law and order
Southeast Asians respect authority, and because of this they respect the law. There is plenty of crime, just as there is anywhere in the world. Con

Opium poppies for making illegal drugs are grown in remote areas in Southeast Asia. In 1989 Thai police had a massive campaign against drugs. They publicly burned millions of pounds worth of opium that they had captured.

artists, thieves, drugpushers, and murderers exist, and there are pirates operating around the islands and off the remote coasts of Thailand. In general, though, Southeast Asians are law-abiding.

All the countries have their own police forces and their own systems of law courts. In most countries the penalties for crime are severe, with long terms of imprisonment. The prisons are harsh and uncomfortable.

The way in which law is maintained in each country largely depends upon the political system. Where the government is efficient, so is the system of justice. In a number of Southeast Asian countries, however, the police are open to corruption; that is to say, the police and lawyers may accept bribes. This may be on a very small scale. For instance, if drivers are stopped by the police for speeding in a car, they might give the police a sum of money and the police would in turn let them go. On a larger, more serious scale, there may be corruption involving large sums of money, illegal drugs, weapons, criminal gangs, and government ministers.

Singapore used to have a serious problem with corruption, but has now succeeded in stamping out most of it. With its strict laws, efficient system of justice, and severe penalties, Singapore now has very little crime. In fact, it is one of the safest places in the world. Only one person out of every 22,000 people in Singapore falls victim to violent crime.

The young and the old

Children are generally well cared for by their parents and also by their older brothers and sisters, aunts and uncles, grandparents, and whoever else is living in the same house or group of houses. At an early age, children are given certain responsibilities. In the country they may have to feed the animals, help in the fields, go on errands to the stores, or collect water from a spring. Girls help to care for any younger children in the family. Children tend to play gently and quietly. They have very few toys. They seem to take their duties seriously and have a sense of being responsible and contributing members of the family and the community to which they belong.

Elderly people also are cared for by the families. They are treated with great respect, and their opinions are always carefully considered. Very old men and women can often be seen doing light work around the house and in the fields, trying to make themselves useful as long as they can. Most people will die in their own homes, attended by their families. There are very few old people's homes.

Education

Since independence, education has been high on the list of priorities in the Southeast Asian nations. When money has been available, school building has flourished. During the 1970s, when the high price of oil brought great wealth to Indonesia, 25,000 primary schools were built.

The governments of all Southeast Asian nations provide free primary education. Some

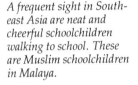

A frequent sight in Southeast Asia are neat and cheerful schoolchildren walking to school. These are Muslim schoolchildren in Malaya.

countries, such as Malaysia and Vietnam, provide free secondary education as well, while others charge a small fee.

In wealthy countries, particularly Singapore, the standards of education are high. Even in the poorer countries, such as Burma, the standard of teaching is good but the schools may be run-down and poorly equipped. In the poorer countries, children may be needed to help in the fields or for other work, and may not be able to continue their education after primary school.

Throughout Southeast Asia, it is common for half the children to attend school in the morning and the other half in the afternoon. This shift system saves money and space.

There are universities and colleges in every country, but the best students are often sent abroad. Some 27,000 Malaysian students study abroad, mainly in the U.S. but also in Canada, Australia, New Zealand, and Britain.

Care for the sick
Health care in Southeast Asia varies enormously. Citizens of Singapore benefit from a well-organized welfare system that provides insurance to cover the costs of medical treatment. Where there is plenty of money, health care is good. However, there is very little money in Cambodia, Burma, and Laos, and consequently health care is very basic.

Indonesia falls between these two extremes. It has some good hospitals and clinics, but health care across the nation varies. The hospitals tend to be for patients with serious injuries and illnesses. There is usually little nursing or rehabilitation. Instead, patients are often cared for by members of their family, who will sit with them, bring them food, wash them, and see that they take their medicine.

In most Southeast Asian countries both Western and traditional kinds of medical practice exist. Hospitals and recently trained doctors follow Western medical practice using surgery, and modern medications. Traditional medical practice uses ancient ideas about how diseases and illnesses can be cured. Many people in Southeast Asia consult traditional doctors and herbalists rather than going to a Western-style doctor or a hospital.

The disease of leprosy is a major problem in tropical countries. This child is being well cared for at a leper colony but hospital facilities vary greatly from area to area and country to country.

80

Traditional Medicine

Many people in Southeast Asia use traditional medicine, often in conjunction with Western-style medicine. Traditional medicine can be used to cure anything from colds to snakebite, from rashes to mental illness. On the simplest level, there are numerous medicines and ointments based on traditional recipes that have been handed down from one generation to the next. They are usually made from local herbs and spices, and are available from market vendors. Medicines may contain strange ingredients, such as snake blood or ground antlers. Massage, especially good for relieving muscular pain and tension, also plays a part in traditional medicine.

For many people in Southeast Asia, religion and health are closely connected. If the body is ill, the soul needs help. Sufferers may go to traditional doctors who use semireligious methods of treatment, perhaps involving chants and magical symbols.

A traditional herbal remedy that is still widely used in Burma is thanaka *bark ointment. It is smeared over the face to protect it from sunburn.*

8 Arts, Crafts, and Leisure

Broadly speaking, life in Southeast Asia is not easy. Living conditions are basic and the food is simple. Most families do not have a car or even a television set. Only the wealthy take vacations.

Despite this, Southeast Asians do like to enjoy life and put their spare time to good use. Many Southeast Asians play sports of various kinds. They are passionate moviegoers. They have a keen sense of beauty in architecture, dance, painting, and sculpture. Most of all, they love festivals, which are held regularly in an atmosphere of colorful, noisy excitement.

Much of traditional Buddhist and Hindu painting portrays scenes from mythology. This wall painting is in the Wat Phra Keo, Bangkok. The action taking place inside the demon's mouth has been painted with typical vigor and imagination.

International sports

Just about any sport you can name is played in Southeast Asia. Soccer is very popular and most villages will have a playing field, even if it is just a flat area of muddy ground. Volleyball, basketball, table tennis and, in particular, badminton are widely played. There are marathons and other athletic events. There are also numerous clubs practicing the martial arts, such as kung fu and karate. Golf, tennis, and the watersports at the beach resorts, such as waterskiing and windsurfing, are played only by the well-to-do Southeast Asians and foreign tourists. There are tenpin bowling alleys in some of the cities. Cricket is played in Singapore and Malaysia, and baseball is played in the Philippines.

Traditional sports

Southeast Asia has its own traditional sports. The rattan ball game called *takraw* in Malay and *chinlon* in Burmese is a delight to watch. The light ball is about the size of a large grapefruit and is made out of woven rattan canes. Six people stand around in a circle and pass the ball to each other using only their legs and head. The object is not to let the ball touch the ground, and to show off the player's graceful, dancelike skills.

Thai-boxing is a professional form of boxing that is still very popular in Thailand. The boxers are allowed to use their feet as well as their gloved hands, delivering sharp kicks to the body.

There is bull racing in Indonesia, in which riders are pulled around the course on little chariots by pairs of hefty buffaloes. Cockfighting is also popular throughout the region, although it

83

A kite flying festival in central Bangkok attracts a large crowd of participants and spectators.

has been officially banned in several countries.

Kite flying is a specialty of the region, particularly in Thailand, Malaysia, and Indonesia. Kites are flown in competitions. Sometimes the kites "fight," the winner being the kite that brings another down. Some kite competitions are judged solely on appearance. These involve magnificent kites, some of them huge and decorated with papier-maché statues and pipes that sing in the wind.

Music and dance

Many of the traditional arts of Southeast Asia have survived in more or less their old form. The classical dancing of Thailand, Cambodia, Java, and Bali is still the same as that used to entertain the courts of the kings and rajas of old. These forms of dance owe their origin to Hindu India. The dancers move about gracefully, twisting and turning their arms and fingers, darting their eyes

Music and dance play a large part in the culture of Southeast Asia and classical dances are still performed at the royal court of Thailand. These classical dancers are highly trained in the skills needed for the traditional stylized movements.

back and forth. The effect is one of great calm, delicacy, and refinement. Tourism has done much to revive an interest in traditional kinds of dancing. Other forms of traditional theatrical entertainment include masked dances, a local kind of opera, and exuberant slapstick pantomime.

The music accompanying these performances has a quite distinctive sound. It is played mainly on xylophonelike instruments, with keys made of metal, wood, or bamboo. To these may be added drums and perhaps a wailing flute or a simple stringed instrument played with a bow.

In the cities, however, the most popular form of music and dancing among young people today is Western-style pop music and disco-dancing.

Arts and crafts

Many of the traditions of skilled handicrafts dating back hundreds of years have survived, and Southeast Asia has numerous active artists, sculptors, and artisans. Crafts have also become an important industry. Carvings, paintings, sculptures, silverware, jewelry, and handwoven cloth are produced in large quantities to sell to visiting tourists and to export to stores abroad. There are large workshops in Java that produce hand-printed cloth called *batik*, a major export product. It is said that five million people in Indonesia alone earn a living from producing and selling crafts.

The world in a screen

Few people actually own televisions in Southeast Asia, but most people know about it. If a village has electricity, then someone will probably have a television, and friends and relatives will crowd around to watch. Many television programs are inferior serials imported from the U.S. and Australia, poorly dubbed in the local language. There are also news programs and, particularly popular, coverage of major sports events. In most of these countries the governments control the television stations and the news programs.

Movies are also very popular. Every small town will have a theater, drawing large and noisy crowds to the shows. The favorite movies are high-action thrillers. The public is informed about what movie is playing by the huge, luridly painted posters that decorate just about every town and city.

There is also another kind of screen entertainment, far more ancient than movies and television: shadow puppets. These puppets are made of flat pieces of buffalo hide, cut and pierced to produce the silhouette of a figure when its shadow is cast on a screen. They are operated from beneath by sticks attached to the limbs. The puppets act out the stories of old folk tales, often with added bits of modern humor. The ancient epic tales of Hindu India, the *Ramayana* and the *Mahabharata*, are still extremely popular in Indonesia and Thailand. A single puppeteer sits behind a screen lit by a flaming oil lamp, performing well into the night, watched by his spellbound audience of young and old alike. He handles a huge cast of characters, each with a different voice; as many as 25 puppets may be on the screen at a time. There are battle scenes, sword fights, clowning, and love scenes. It is the very same mix of subjects, in fact, that is now so popular in the movies.

Festivals

The Southeast Asians love festivals. These are times when families and friends gather, often in their best clothes, for feasts, parades, music, and dancing. Most of the festivals of the region center upon religious events, although Independence Day is also celebrated with festivals and a public holiday in most countries.

All over Southeast Asia festivals are frequent, brightly colored, and lively. In Thailand decorated barges are used when the king travels to Wat Arun, the Temple of Dawn.

The Philippines is the land of the *fiesta*, colorful and dramatic festivals of Spanish origin, but with very distinctive local touches. They are held by individual towns and villages to celebrate their patron saint. These are spectacular occasions, calling for the finest outfits and fancy dress and

lavish street decorations. Statues of the saints are paraded through the streets in passionate processions, after which everyone launches into generous feasting and high-spirited fun.

In Malaysia, Hindus celebrate the annual festival of Thaipusam at shrines set in huge limestone caves. Devotees of the Hindu deity Murugan go into a blissful trance and then have spikes and hooks inserted into their bodies, even right through their cheeks. This apparently causes little pain, and there is little loss of blood. The devotees make their way up to the shrine, encouraged by the roar of the huge crowd. Despite the way it appears to Westerners, this is a joyful occasion.

In complete contrast, in Thailand, Loy Krathong is celebrated at the full moon during November. In the evening thousands of people go quietly to the lakes and rivers with tiny boats made of banana leaves. In the boats they put a candle and a stick of incense and then set them afloat. Some say that the festival is in honor of the gods, some say it cleanses people of their sins, while others say it is a time to make wishes.

The Chinese celebrate their New Year in Singapore with feasting and parades. These include the famous dragon dances, in which the great masks and cloth bodies of the dragons are skillfully made to writhe by teams of men inside. In Bali there are estimated to be some 35,000 different temple festivals in a year, many of them accompanied by music and dance and beautiful displays of offerings of fruit and flowers for the gods.

9 Southeast Asia on the Rise

Southeast Asia is one of the few regions that are able to face the rapid changes and pressures of today's world in an atmosphere of prosperity. The region can feed itself; its land is also rich in minerals, oil, and timber. Its people are able to produce high-quality industrial goods, from clothing to digital watches. Southeast Asia has attracted the interest of many international businesses and has received large injections of valuable foreign investment. Tourists from all over the world come to its beaches and islands, to enjoy its food and its festivals, and to visit its great historical monuments.

Not all the countries of Southeast Asia have been able to follow the path to prosperity. Nonetheless, the region as a whole promises to be one of the most interesting and dynamic in the world over the coming decades.

Rich and poor
Southeast Asia contains enormous contrasts between wealth and poverty. The ASEAN countries have shown how Southeast Asia can prosper. They have achieved this through political stability and by encouraging investment in their industries from abroad. By relating to each other as a group, they now see their problems as regional ones that they can solve by working together. If their economies continue to improve steadily, there is a real chance that all

In Southeast Asia there is a fast-growing population and many areas are very crowded, as this busy street in Rangoon, Burma, shows. There is often very real poverty and not everyone shares in the growing prosperity of many regions.

their people will benefit, narrowing the gap between the rich and poor.

A threatened environment

All the Southeast Asian countries suffer from rapidly expanding populations. Thailand's population has tripled in the last 50 years. Indonesia had a population of 38 million in 1905, 153 million in 1982, and is expected to have 212 million by the year 2000. Almost all the countries of the region have had to introduce family planning programs to try to encourage couples to have no more than two children each.

The rise in population is putting increasing pressure on the ecology of Southeast Asia. Rural areas around the towns and cities are being

91

Rapidly expanding cities, such as Manila in the Philippines, constantly encroach on farmland or forest and create pollution. They are also often the center for demonstrations and riots in times of political troubles.

developed. The air is becoming increasingly polluted by exhaust fumes and industrial waste. Forests are being overexploited for their timber and the seas are being overfished.

The ASEAN countries have recognized the need to do something about these problems. Only in the coming decades will we know if ASEAN has succeeded in saving its rich resources from permanent damage.

Peace and prosperity

The Southeast Asian nations can only prosper in an atmosphere of political stability. They depend on trade with the rest of the world, but foreign trading partners are not eager to do business with countries that show signs of instability.

Life in Southeast Asia is changing quickly but alongside the new ideas many traditions continue to remain. These Buddhist monks are still very much part of life in Thailand, where most men and boys become monks for short periods in their life and then return to their families.

Southeast Asia has not rid itself completely of the problems that have faced it since World War II and independence. The government of the Philippines still suffers from occasional efforts by army units to overthrow it, while Communist and Muslim guerrillas operate in the countryside and in the southern islands. Vietnam still has a hard-line Communist government, under which the economy has failed to flourish. The Boat People continue to flood out of Vietnam, desperate to find a better life elsewhere in the world. In Cambodia, the Khmer Rouge threaten civil war against their fellow citizens. Thailand still has to play host to thousands of refugees from Vietnam and Cambodia. Burma is still recovering from a year of riots in 1988. Numerous Burmese citizens who have spoken out against the military

93

government have been put in prison. Meanwhile in the border regions a number of tribal groups are fighting a guerrilla war for their independence.

Southeast Asia still has many troubles of this kind. It can be said, however, that it has fewer troubles today than it did 30, or 20, or even just ten years ago.

Unity and diversity

ASEAN has done much to give Southeast Asia a sense of its own identity. This identity, however, is not just a question of political outlook or economics. There are clearly many other things that the Southeast Asian countries share that set them apart from the rest of the world.

Foreigners notice this as soon as they step off a plane. There is the smell of the humid air, the fragrant and spicy food, the tropical fruit, the greenness of the landscape, the heady scent of the frangipani blossom. The people have delicate features and unusual grace. They represent a unique mixture of cultures that have blended together over centuries: Hindu and Buddhist, Islamic, Christian, Malay, Chinese, Indian, and European.

All these things help to reinforce the idea that Southeast Asia is not just a handful of separate countries hanging off one corner of Asia, but a region with a distinct character and a major contribution to make to the world. The motto of Indonesia is *Bhinneka Tunggal Ika*, which means "Unity in Diversity." It might also be the motto of Southeast Asia as a whole.

Index

Laos 5, 12, 44–45
law and order 75–77

Malay Peninsula 5, 20, 23, 25, 37
Malaysia 5, 7, 37–38, 42, 75
Marcos, Ferdinand 42–43, 74
Mekong River 12
migrant workers 33–34, 44, 57
mining and minerals 15, 33, 52
monsoons 10
mountains 12–13
  Mt. Djaja (highest) 12
movies and television 86–88
music and dance 85–86

New Guinea 7

orangutans 15
overseas investment 48–49

Pagan 24–25, 54
Penan people 73
petroleum and gas 53
Philippines 7, 29–30, 35, 36, 42–
  44, 74–75, 93
plantations 33–34, 49–50
plants 14–15
pollution 92
population 8, 91
Portuguese empire 28–29
poverty 44, 56–58

Rangoon (Yangon) 12
religion 20–23, 25–26, 29, 62–64,
  89
remote peoples 71–73
rice 10–11, 49, 68–71

rivers 11–12, 66
rubber 34, 50

shipping 23, 59
Singapore 7, 32, 38, 58–60, 75, 77
Spice Islands 28–29
spice trade 20, 27–29, 50
sports 83–84
standard of living 55–57, 60
Suharto, President 42, 74
Sukarno, President 37, 42, 74
Sulawesi 7, 71–72
Sumatra 7, 23

Thailand 5, 32, 75, 91, 93
timber trade 51–52
Toraja people 71–72
tourism 53–55
trade 19–20, 23, 32–33
transportation 11–12, 55

United States 35–36, 38–39, 40–
41

Vietnam 5, 38–40, 41–42, 93
  Vietnam War 38–40
village life 61–62, 66–68
volcanoes 12–13

West Irian (Irian Jaya) 7, 37
wildlife 15–17
World War II 35–36

© Heinemann Children's Reference 1991
Originally published 1991 by Heinemann
Children's Reference, a division of
Heinemann Educational Books, Ltd.